KU-012-582

Tigers

James Maclaine

Designed by Sam Chandler

Illustrated by John Francis and Kimberley Scott

Tiger consultant: Professor David Macdonald CBE,
Wildlife Conservation Research Unit, University of Oxford

Reading consultant: Alison Kelly, Principal Lecturer at the University of Roehampton

Contents

CROYDON LIBRARIES

ASH

3 8015 02366 942 1

ASKEWS & HOLT | 13-Jul-2012

J599.756 JUNIOR | £4.99

Super cats

Tigers are the heaviest, longest and strongest wild cats in the world.

Most tigers have orange and white fur with dark stripes.

Each tiger has its own pattern of stripes.

Some tigers have white fur with stripes. They only survive in zoos.

Tiger homes

Tigers live in forests, mountains or swamps.

Some tigers live where it's hot. Others live where it's cold.

This is a Siberian tiger. It has very thick fur that keeps it warm in the snow.

Adult tigers live alone. Each tiger lives in its own area of land known as its territory.

A tiger chooses a place with plenty of trees and bushes, so it can hide.

Each territory needs rivers or pools where a tiger can drink.

There should also be lots of animals living in the area for the tiger to eat.

Smelly cats

Tigers mark their territories with smells, to show that they live there.

Tigers scratch trees and rub in scent from their paws.

They also spray on rocks and trees in their territories.

These tigers are sniffing a rock that another tiger has marked.

This tiger is marking a tree. It's rubbing scent from its cheek onto the trunk.

Tigers also mark where they live with piles of dung.

On the hunt

Tigers hunt animals for food. They often hunt when it's dark.

A tiger quietly follows a group of deer. Slowly, it creeps up on them.

When it's close to the group, the tiger quickly runs at the nearest deer.

It knocks the deer down to the ground. Then, the tiger bites its throat.

Tigers hide in tall grasses and bushes while they hunt.

This Bengal tiger is hiding in long grass. The stripes on its fur make it hard for other animals to spot.

Tigers use their good hearing to help them hunt. They can hear five times better than people.

Meat eaters

Tigers mostly eat other animals such as deer, cows and wild pigs.

They sometimes eat smaller animals and fish, too.

This Siberian tiger is hunting in a river.

When a tiger has killed an animal, it drags its body somewhere safe.

The tiger chews away any hair with its teeth. Then, it eats the meat.

Later, it uses its rough tongue to lick any meat left on the bones.

Now and then, tigers eat grass to stay healthy.

Teeth and claws

Tigers have very sharp teeth and claws. They keep them strong and clean by chewing and scratching wood.

This young tiger is chewing on a stick, to clean its teeth.

A tiger's biggest teeth are longer than your fingers.

Tigers keep their claws safe inside their paws, but they push them out when they dig, fight or scratch.

This Siberian tiger is using its claws to hold on as it climbs up a tree trunk.

Quiet time

Tigers spend a large part of the day resting and sleeping.

This Bengal tiger is asleep on a cool, rocky ledge.

Each tiger has several dens. These are caves or bushes where it likes to rest.

A tiger also rests next to its food, to stop other animals from eating it.

Tigers sometimes rest in pools, so that flies can't bite their bodies.

Sometimes, a tiger just lies down in a patch of grass and goes to sleep.

After a tiger has woken up, it stretches its legs, neck and back.

Keep out!

Tigers try to keep other tigers out of their territories.

When a tiger meets another tiger in its territory, it stares fiercely at it.

Next, it hisses, growls and shows its teeth, to scare away the other tiger.

If the other tiger doesn't leave, they might fight.

Tigers use their sharp claws to hurt each other when they fight. Sometimes, they fight until one tiger is killed.

If a tiger is hurt in a fight, it licks its wounds to clean them.

Tiger cubs

Baby tigers are called cubs. A female tiger has two to four cubs at a time.

Cubs are born with their eyes shut. They open them after two weeks.

The young cubs stay close to their mother's body to keep warm.

For the first two months, the cubs only drink their mother's milk.

The stripes on a tiger cub's
fur become darker over time.

These tiger cubs have blue eyes. Their
eyes will turn orange as they get older.

Growing up

Tiger cubs live with their mother for a few years. The mother takes care of the cubs and teaches them how to survive.

A mother tiger leads her cubs around her territory.

She takes them to water so they can drink.

She also shows them how to hide while hunting.

Tiger cubs become better hunters by playing with each other.

These cubs are learning how to use their bodies and paws while play-fighting.

Water cats

Unlike most other cats, tigers enjoy spending time in water.

Tigers are very good swimmers, but they prefer to keep their heads above water.

Tigers swim fast because they have big, flat paws.

This tiger is resting in a pool. Tigers lie in shallow water to cool down when it's hot.

They chase other animals into rivers while hunting, to slow them down.

After spending time in water, tigers dry their fur by shaking their heads and bodies.

Keeping clean

Tigers keep clean by licking dirt and loose hairs from their fur.

This Sumatran tiger is cleaning its leg with its rough tongue.

A tiger can't lick most of its own face, but it can still keep it clean.

The tiger licks the back of its paw...

...and rubs it up and down its face.

A mother tiger washes her cubs by licking them.

Tiger talk

Tigers tell each other things by making noises and moving their heads and bodies.

When a female tiger wants to attract a male, she roars very loudly.

If a tiger is angry, it snarls and swishes its tail quickly from side to side.

A mother tiger hisses and growls at her cubs if they annoy her.

Tigers display the backs of their ears when they're trying to scare each other.

These Siberian tigers are greeting each other by rubbing their heads together.

Tigers in trouble

There used to be lots of tigers living in the wild, but people hunted them and destroyed their territories.

Today, there are fewer than 4,000 tigers in the wild. People are trying to find out where they live, so they can protect them.

Special cameras are put on trees in places where people think tigers live.

If an animal walks past the tree, the camera takes a photograph.

This photo shows a tiger walking through its territory at night.

Its territory is in a protected part of India where tigers can live safely.

Glossary

Here are some of the words in this book you might not know. This page tells you what they mean.

 swamp - an area of wet land partly covered with water.

 territory - an area of land where an animal lives.

 mark - to leave a smell. Tigers mark places to show where they live.

 hunt - to search for, catch and kill animals, usually to eat.

 claw - a long and sharp nail that an animal uses to scratch.

 den - a place where an animal likes to rest or sleep.

 cub - a baby tiger. Mother tigers have two to four cubs.

Websites to visit

You can visit exciting websites to find out more about tigers.

To visit these websites, go to the Usborne Quicklinks Website at **www.usborne-quicklinks.com** Read the internet safety guidelines, and then type the keywords "**beginners tigers**".

The websites are regularly reviewed and the links in Usborne Quicklinks are updated. However, Usborne Publishing is not responsible, and does not accept liability, for the content or availability of any website other than its own. We recommend that children are supervised while on the internet.

Tigers have short, powerful legs that help them to jump.

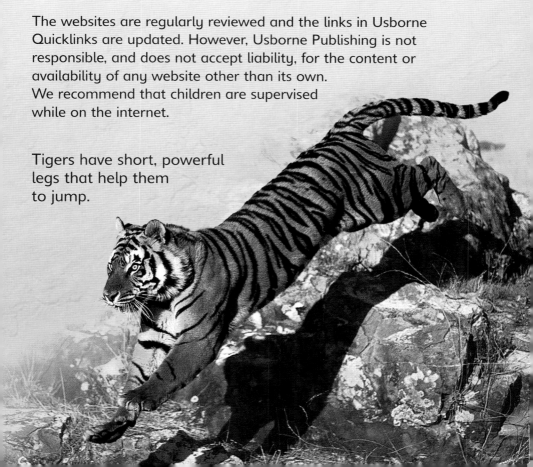

Index

Acknowledgements

Photographic manipulation by John Russell

Photo credits
The publishers are grateful to the following for permission to reproduce material:
cover © **DLILLC/Corbis/photolibrary.com**; p1 © **DLILLC/Corbis/SuperStock**; p2-3 © **Theo Allofs/ Minden Pictures/SuperStock**; p4 © **Konrad Wothe/Minden Pictures/SuperStock**; p6 © **Chris Brunskill/ ardea.com**; p7 © **J-L. Klein & M-L. Hubert/Bios/photolibrary.com**; p9 © **Pierre Vernay/Bios/ photolibrary.com**; p10 © **Belinda Images/SuperStock**; p12 © **imagebroker.net/SuperStock**; p13 © **Tom & Pat Leeson/ardea.com**; p14-15 © **Thorsten Milse/Mauritius/photolibrary.com**; p16 © **Vivek Sharma/Foto Natura/Minden Pictures/SuperStock**; p17 © **Andy Rouse/NaturePL/SuperStock**; p19 © **Schafer & Hill/Peter Arnold Images/photolibrary.com**; p21 © **Renee Lynn/CORBIS**; p22 © **Stéphanie Meng/Bios/photolibrary.com**; p23 © **David Woodfall/SuperStock**; p24-25 © **Mark Newman/Age fotostock/photolibrary.com**; p27 © **DLILLC/Corbis/SuperStock**; p28-29 © **Steve Winter/National Geographic/Getty Images**; p31 © **DLILLC/Corbis/SuperStock**

Every effort has been made to trace and acknowledge ownership of copyright. If any rights have been omitted, the publishers offer to rectify this in any subsequent editions following notification.

First published in 2012 by Usborne Publishing Ltd., Usborne House, 83-85 Saffron Hill, London EC1N 8RT, England. www.usborne.com Copyright © 2012 Usborne Publishing Ltd. The name Usborne and the devices ♀♥ are Trade Marks of Usborne Publishing Ltd. All rights reserved. No part of this publication may be reproduced, stored in a retrieval system, or transmitted in any form or by any means, electronic, mechanical, photocopying, recording or otherwise without the prior permission of the publisher. First published in America 2012. U.E.

Sun, moon and stars

Farm animals

Elizabeth I

RUBBISH AND RECYCLING

Dogs

Horses and ponies

Spiders

Planes

Ancient Greeks

Cats

VOLCANOES

DINOSAURS

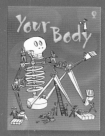
Your Body

Armour

Sharks

Celts

Vikings

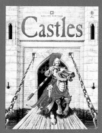
Castles

How flowers grow

Digging up the past

Living in space

Caterpillars and Butterflies

Ballet

Pirates

Egyptians

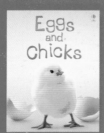

Eggs and Chicks

Romans

Weather

Tadpoles and Frogs

Why do we eat?

Under the sea

Bears

Aztecs

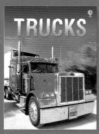

TRUCKS

Night Animals

Firefighters

Antarctica

Bugs

COWBOYS

Planet Earth